Greenholm Remembered

by M Warwick

1. COPY OF THE COVER OF THE ORIGINAL

1988

CONTENTS

PART ONE

ORIGINAL ACKNOWLEDGEMENTS 1988

This account of Greenholme Mills could not have been produced without the assistance of a number of people in Burley-in-Wharfedale. I wish to thank the former mill workers who agreed to talk about their working lives, together with the members of the W.E.A. Class who interviewed them.

In addition I should like to thank David James of the Bradford Archives Department, for allowing members of the class to use documents from the Fison collection in the Ilkley Library and the Library Staff for their assistance. Some searches through the local newspapers have been made in the Ilkley Library but also in the offices of the *Wharfedale and Airedale Observer*. I wish to thank the staff of the reporters' office who have always been willing to arrange visits and answer enquiries.

Finally I wish to thank Mary Hill and Ella Stradling for reading the rough copy of the text and Gena Lodge for typing it out. Some of the photographs are from a 1927 pamphlet reprinted from *Town and Country News*, which was kindly lent by Dennis Williams, together with the visiting card used for the front cover. The photograph, taken in the 1920s, of workers and former workers outside the mill was lent by Arthur Taylor, and that of the women workers in 1966 by Annie Metcalf.

Members of the W.E.A. Joint Tutorial Class from 1983 to 1986, who helped in various ways with the original interviews and with the research were: Sylvia Baty, Jim Bennett. John Breare, Joanne Breare, Gladys Ellwood, Ruby Hardaker, Marjorie Kell, Gill Kilner, Bruce Kirkbright, Elizabeth Macalister, Mary Maeso, Carole Mumford, Geoffrey Rowson, Lucie Wright and the co-tutor, Dennis Warwick.

Margaret Warwick 1988

ORIGINAL INTRODUCTION 1988

Over twenty years have elapsed since William Fison and Company ceased trading at Greenholme Mills, Burley-in-Wharfedale but the large multi-storeyed stone buildings remain standing as a visible reminder of the industry on which the local economy once depended. There are still many people who are now middle aged or older, who remember working at Fison's prior to the firm's closure in October 1966. The reminiscences contained in this study are intended to give some insight into the working lives of these former employees.

Members of a Workers' Educational Association Local Studies Group in the early 1980s arranged to interview men and women in the village who had started to work at Greenholme during World War I. My own conversations with others who started working in the 1920s and 1930s brought together later memories of the mills. Additional information on the firm's history is based on work which the Group did in reading the Company's papers in the Bradford Archives and researching in the files of the two local newspapers, the *Ilkley Gazette* and the *Wharfedale and Airedale Observer*. Statistical information on population and employment figures has been taken mainly from the Census reports for Burley-in-Wharfedale.

2. Greenholme Mills from the path beside the Goit. This photo appeared in a feature article on Fisons in *Town and Country News* in 1927.

THE MILL VILLAGE

Throughout the nineteenth century and for the first half of the twentieth century, Burley was essentially a mill village. Cotton manufacturing in the early nineteenth century was superseded by worsted production in 1850, after William Fison and William Edward Forster bought Greenholme mills. In the third quarter of the nineteenth century, the prosperous years for the worsted trade, approximately 60 percent of Burley's total workforce were listed as textile operatives on the census returns. By 1881 the proportion had begun to drop and just less than 50 percent were in mill work[1]. In the early decades of the twentieth century the proportion had dropped still further, to 28 percent in 1921[2] and 27 percent in 1931[3]. Textile work was, however, still the predominant occupation in 1931. Agriculture occupied 5 percent of the total workforce, building and related trades 5.4 percent, shops and distributive trades 11.7 percent and local government 11.3 percent.

3. William Fison stood at the door of Greenholme about 1896.

4. William Edward Forster, c. 1870 when he was M.P. for Bradford.

Total numbers employed at Greenholme mills at any one time are difficult to ascertain. The surviving Company papers give no information; the census returns which refer to Burley village give no indication as to whether textile workers list were working at Greenholme or elsewhere; the number who travelled into Burley to work is also impossible to estimate. Trade Directories, though not always an accurate source of information do give some clues. According to Kelly's Directories, one thousand people were employed at Greenholme mills in 1871, 800 in 1877 and 700 in the years 1889 and 1908. Subsequent Directories unfortunately give no such figures but like that on 1917 only refer to the fact that 'the inhabitants of Burley are chiefly employed in spinning and manufacturing worsted'.[4]

According to Directory information, therefore, there were probably about 700 people at Greenholme mills during World War I, when the 80 year olds who were interviewed first started work. Employment was easy to find in the mills during the 1914-18 war. Firms such as Fison's were expected to increase their output to meet government contracts for textiles. Uncertainties and losses which had been experienced in the trade in the pre-war years were temporarily forgotten and large profits were made.

Once the war-time boom ended, however, falling demands at home and abroad, coupled with renewed foreign competition, meant severe problems for the textile trade. Losses increased in the 1920s until the firm's overdraft stood at £70,000 in 1927[5]. Five years later Barclay's Bank refused to support further borrowing by the Company[6]. Drastic reorganisation became imperative and was carried out under the new chairmanship of J. Horace Lockwood from 1932. The whole of the firm's property was mortgaged to the more accommodating Midland Bank and strict controls were imposed on spending. The firm managed to stagger on through the slump of the 1930s and again profited by war-time contracts in World War II.

5. J. Horace Lockwood M.P.

The people interviewed can remember many of the changes which took place during the later years of the firm's existence. For instance, they recalled the periods of short time working in the 1930s but the long hours of overtime necessary in World War II. Those who remained in the 1950s remembered the introduction of new machinery, new working practices and synthetic fibres. Despite the efforts made to modernise, cutbacks continued. By the 1960s the textile trade throughout the West Riding was facing mounting difficulties particularly from overseas competition and Fisons was one of the many firms which was forced to close. The Company finally ceased to operate in October 1966.

6. An artist's impression of Greenhome mills from the journal *Filaments* dated 1962. The L-shaped block in the foreground was gutted by fire in 1966.

EMPLOYMENT IN BURLEY

The majority of village children in the early twentieth century would expect to start their working lives at Greenholme mills. We know that in 1881, from Census of that year, that 62 percent of all the girls in the 12 to 15 age group were listed as textile workers and 68 percent of all the boys in that age group[7]. All those interviewed had started to work part-time at age 12 and at 13 had become full-time employees working a 55 hour week. Mr. A. was an exception. Having done well at school, and because war-time (1914-18) relaxations in employment regulations, he was 'allowed' to start full-time work at 12. Not until after 1918, when the school leaving age was raised to 14 and half-time work was officially ended, were the numbers of young adolescents employed at the mill substantially reduced.

Between the two World Wars, the choice of employment for the majority of working class women and girls in the village was still that of textile work or domestic service. The published 1921 Census Employment Statistics revealed that 45 percent of the employed women in Burley were in textiles and 28 percent were involved in paid domestic work. Only 5 percent were occupied in commerce and 4 percent were dressmakers or milliners[8]. At the time of the 1931 Census, which was a bad year for the textile industry, the percentage of employed women and girls listed as textile workers was reduced to 38 percent with a slightly larger proportion than before in domestic work. A number of those interviewed suggested that despite the long hours and monotony of much of the mill work, it was preferred to the less well paid and more lonely drudgery of domestic service.

Once a woman married, she was expected to give up her job and stay at home. Very few women whose husbands were in paid employment had ever been employed at Greenholme mills after marriage. This was evident in the Census returns. In 1881 only 7 percent of women textile workers were married and half of these were in the 20 to 29 age group[9]. During World War I there was a break with this tradition when more hands were required, but in the 1920s and 30s the married women returned to unpaid household chores. According to Miss B. wives who worked when their husbands were also employed, risked being classes as ‘greedy’ by their neighbours and other workers.

For male workers during the inter-war period, textiles, printing engineering, agriculture, commerce and local government provided the main areas of employment. In 1921, 19.7 percent were classed as textile workers, 13.5 percent as metal workers, 12.4 percent as agricultural workers, and 9.3 percent were in commerce. Ten years later the census reveals that 21 percent were in textiles, only 6.8 percent in engineering and more had moved into the commercial and distributive trades and local government[11]. In the worst of the depression years of the early 1930s, it seems likely that some men accepted work in the mills which they might previously have rejected. One of the women interviewees, Mrs C., knew of men being taken on to work a night shift at Greenholme in the spinning department and remembers how they resented having to do what was traditionally 'women's work'.

7. The weir. When the river was dammed in 1796 it provided the power to drive mill machinery. A goit led the water to the mills. The first dam was swept away in a flood, and the one in this photograph was built in 1810. (see p. 32)

WORKING AT GREENHOLME MILLS

Most of the young employees in the early twentieth century, including those we interviewed, worked initially in the spinning departments at the mills. Young doffers like Mr. D. would remove the full bobbins from the frames; others, of whom Mr. A. was one, would be piecers, joining together the delicate threads. Girls working on the spinning frames would start off with a few bobbins at first, gradually increasing the number when they became more accustomed to the process. Prior to 1919, work started at 6 am when all the machines were turned on. Before work began on dark winter mornings, Miss E. Remembers snatching a few precious moments to rest, using the big boxes at one end of the room to sit on. The rats and mice which had a free run of the place during the night soon disappeared when the lights went up and the machinery began to clatter. Like many others, Miss E. will never forget the shattering noise of the spinning frames which made communication, other than lip reading, virtually impossible. She also recalls how terrified she was of the overlooker who shouted at his young charges in a fearsome voice. If they stayed at the mill in the spinning section, young doffers could progress to become head doffers in charge of a group of other youngsters, spinners or possibly twisters*.

8. A group of overlookers at Greenholme Mills in the 1930s.

Back row L to R: Jim Mounsey, John Shuttleworth, John Breare, Albert Herrin and Mr. Worsnop (superviser).

Front L to R.: John Herrin, Norman Overin, Powell Calvert

After two or three years as spinners, two of the women

interviewed had paid ten shillings for tuition which gave them the opportunity to transfer to skilled jobs in the weaving sheds. Ten shillings was a considerable sum of money when it is remembered that young workers were only earning 3shillings and 9 pence a week as half-timers or 8 shillings and 6 pence for a full 55 hour week.

Weavers were paid 'by the piece', which was a 70 yard length of cloth. In order to count for payment of wages on Friday, the piece had to be ready by the end of the working day on Thursday. Miss B recalls that the vagaries of the weather sometimes had a disastrous effect on a weaver's output. When the river Wharfe was low, the water powered turbines ran more slowly and so did the looms which they powered. In these circumstances completion of the 70 yards became exceedingly difficult. Pieces varied in the amount of expertise required in the weaving and therefore a skilled operative, allocated a difficult assignment by the overlooker, could be hard pressed to 'get the pent up'[12] by the Thursday deadline. The overlookers' powers over the workers were considerable, particularly in the allocation of work and the checking of a finished piece. Skilled adult weavers on piece work could expect to earn about 27 shillings a week in the late 1930s; Miss B. Remembers receiving 12 shillings a week as a trainee at this period.

An apprenticeship in burling and mending was a means of further improving status and wages for some women workers. Skilled burlers and menders were the best paid of the female work force and by the very nature of their job had to be accommodated in clean and well-lit rooms. Miss G. Remembers 40 girls being involved in the work in the 1920s. Pieces of cloth varied so much in the skill and time required to perfect them (which was the work of the burlers and menders) that they were all costed separately and some might take a full week to complete.

The firm was well known in the early years of the twentieth century for its 'true blue serges'. Our informants, however,

9. The burlers and menders at Greenholme mills in 1937 (coronation year).

commented on the fact that Fisons wove the cloth 'in the gray' and sent it away for dyeing. The serge was suitable for use in ladies' and gents' suits and for more hard wearing purposes. Orders from the Manchester and Liverpool police forces, for instance, were noted in the firm's Minute Books, and the Canadian Mounties were reputed to have been supplied with Fison's serge. Former weavers also remember the showerproof light tropical suiting which was a speciality of the late 1920s and 30s, and the mohair pile fabrics produced for cinema seats and the growing market in saloon car upholstery[13].

Rather than concentrating on the technical details of the work processes, those who were interviewed p referred to talk more about the number of hours they worked and the conditions under which they worked. A minimum of 55½ hours a week seems to have been normal in the 1914-18 war years. The day commenced at 6 a.m. and continued till 5.30 p.m. on weekdays. An hour was allowed for lunch and thirty minutes for breakfast.

A 5½ hour shift on Saturday mornings completed the working week. At least two of those interviewed considered that they had done a 57 hour week in the early days. In 1919, however, hours of work in the textile trade were reduced by national agreement and a 48 hour week became normal[14]. Work then began at 7.15 a.m. and continued till 5.30 p.m. on weekdays and 11.40 a.m. on Saturdays. Mr. A. Remembers the dinner hour break being reduced by two minutes so that work could finish by 11.30 a.m. on Saturdays without loss of time to the firm. A mill buzzer was sounded five minutes before the commencement of work both in the mornings and afternoons. The large iron gates were always closed exactly on time and late-comers would be duly identified as they passed through the side gate.

Workers came to the Burley mills from the surrounding areas notably Ilkley, Otley and Menston, and our informants remember the works' vehicles fitted with wooden bench seats which brought in the outsiders in the 1920s and 1930s. Unlike the majority of Greenholme's workers, they had to stay on the premises during the midday break, availing themselves of hot drinks from the canteen or the meals which could be bought for about 10d. (4p). Facilities for washing during the long day were minimal as in most work places in the early twentieth century. The soap provided by the firm was, according to Miss F. the same as that used in the wool scouring process and contained a large amount of soda. Not surprisingly most of the girls brought their own soap.

Workers had to provide their own 'protective' clothing. Spinners wore long 'pinnies' which could be bought at a local shop for 1s 11d. (9p) in the 1930s. Weavers had all-embracing overalls but did not tend to get so dirty at work as those who were in the spinning departments. Miss F. remembers how difficult it was to remove mohair and camel-hair fluff from clothes. Khaki was also remembered for the excessive amount of fluff which was shed during its production in World War I. The firm merely provided extra buckets of water to enable the girls to wet their hands and remove the fluff from their clothes as best they

10. Sorting mohair for car upholstery.

11. A spinning room.

Photos 9 to 12 were used in a feature article in *Town and Country News* in 1927.

could. Even the sorters whose work on the fleeces exposed them

12. A combing shed

13. Looms in a weaving shed

The article also showed photos of Fison's offices in Bradford and London.

to the possibility of anthrax infection, provided their own blue and white check 'brats'[15] which had to be washed weekly at home. Mrs C. Remembers the thick grease which had to be scraped off before it was possible to start washing her father's 'brat'.

For those involved in office work at Greenholme, life could be more varied. Mr. A. for instance, whose father was an overlooker, started to work as a 'piecer' in 1915 but was transferred to the General Office at the end of World War I. He could not recollect applying for, or even wanting to transfer, the arrangement had been made between his father and the management. His duties included one of accompanying a somewhat elderly employee to Barclay's Bank (in the village then) at the same time each week in order to collect the cash for Friday's wage packets. They brought all the money from the bank (next to today's pharmacy) back along Main Street and down Iron Row in a hand-cart.

Another of his duties was to collect the rents each Monday from houses owned by Fisons in Main Street, North View, Spring Gardens, Park Row and Iron Row. This task occupied him for most of the day. Mr. H. remembered his days as an office boy when, as was typical of the time, all the clerks worked at high desks and stools. A strict discipline was maintained in the office over the boys and cleanliness was expected at all times. In this connection, regular inspections were made to ensure the boys had cleaned their finger nails. It was not surprising that he welcomed the chance to leave the office for two or three days. He recalled how he used to look forward to accompanying the buyer on his annual round of Dales' farms to purchase fleeces for the firm. Journeys in the work's vehicle were slow in the 1920s and overnight stops were necessary at selected farms along the route.

During all the conversations with former mill employees, the worries of the depression years were most vividly remembered. Short time working and wage reductions affected most of those who were interviewed; unemployment and the dole were even harsher realities for some of them. Fisons first reduced wages and salaries for all their employees at Greenholme mills and Parkside mills in Bradford, in May 1929. A notice was posted up at Greenholme which referred to the 'severe and unfair competition posed by imported yarns and piece goods'. The Chairman at that time, W. H. Arnold-Forster, pointed out that the Directors and Heads of Department had already agreed to their cut and hoped that the work-people would do the same, 'as there is no other alternative'[16]. Burley's 600 employees did accept the 1s 6d in the £1 loss of wages which the cut entailed but not so the 150 at Parkside who went on strike[17]. Their action was possibly a last desperate protest. The firm was already planning closure of the loss making spinning enterprise in Bradford once the lease on the property ran out at the end of they year. Further wage cuts at Greenholme are referred to in the firm's Minute Books in May 1931. Again there is no reference to any organised resistance. Union activity at Burley's mill was virtually non-existent at this period. Only an Overlookers' Union was remembered by one of those interviewed. Bradford's textile workers were reputed to have been much more involved in Union activity than those in Burley.

While those working in textiles were having to accept wage cuts, there were others who were unemployed in Burley at this time. The summary tables for the 1931 Census record that 96men and 26 women in Burley were 'out of work' in the early months of that year, or just over 7 percent of the total workforce in the village[18]. There is no way of knowing how many of the122 unemployed were textile operatives, or how many from other trades and industries. Two years later, in February 1933, the *Ilkley Gazette* gave the number of unemployed or partially employed in Burley as approximately 200. Their plight prompted a public meeting to be held and an 'ad hoc' Unemployment Committee to be formed to co-ordinate welfare efforts[19]. Twenty four allotments were made available to those out of work; welfare rooms in the Victoria Hall (it stood where the Scout Hut stands in Peel Place now) were opened up and an appeal made for suitable furniture; physical education classes were started, especially for unemployed young men; in addition distress vouchers were 2s 6d were distributed to eight needy families each week[20]. One Burley villager remembers how at this time her father, a skilled wool sorter, had walked to and from Bradford calling at 26 mills vainly trying to obtain work. She has never forgotten the sight of his blistered and swollen feet after that fruitless journey.

In the second half of 1933, there was a slight improvement in Fison's trading position. The *Ilkley Gazette* noted in mid June the resumption of a night shift at Greenholme and an increase in the number of wool combers at work there, compared with earlier in the year[21]. At the beginning of September, the Council's Unemployment Committee reported that only 20 were unemployed and six previously unemployed committee members were all in work. The emergency schemes were discontinued though all the allotment holders were allowed to continue cultivating their land[22].

Short time working remained a constant worry until the end of the 1930s, and various periods of slack or short time were remembered by those interviewed. Some recalled working for three days at the mill and then signing on for their wages to be made up in dole money. Signing on for the dole and signing off meant a journey to the Unemployment Office in Otley. Walking there saved the 2d bus fare but frequent walks were hard on shoe leather.

Though not personally affected by unemployment or short time working in the 1930s, Mr. A., an office worker, remembers the very different atmosphere which was apparent as soon as Horace Lockwood became Chairman of the company in 1932. The Fison and Forster families, though still represented on

14. This photograph was probably taken on an occasion in the late 1920s when former employees had been invited back to the mills. Members of the senior management are seen hatless standing on the iron staircase in the background. The Company Accountant, H. Jeffrey is half way up the staircase, next down is W. H. Arnold-Forster, Chairman from 1925 to 1932 and below them are J. Mason Thomas, Company Secretary, W.H. Mitchell, Guy Fison and E.G.H. Mitchell (all Directors).

The just visible letters COCK on the board above the Directors are part of the name board of the Cockatoo Company, which was a registered subsidiary from 1916. It was a mail order type business and according to one of its brochures dealt in dress and coat materials by the yard, cashmere and mohair shawls and speciality wools and yarns. (Photo supplied by Arthur Taylor.)

the Board, ceased from that time onwards to wield their once customary paternal influence over mill and village affairs. Mr. Lockwood was determined to undertake a thorough overhaul of the whole establishment in a bid to keep the firm in business.

Working practices in all departments were scrutinised and no details seemed to have escaped his supervision. For instance in Mr. A's office staff were warned that 'promiscuous writing of letters was to cease'[23], and one of the Directors, E.G. Mitchell, was to be held responsible for all correspondence. From the outset many Greenholme workers distrusted Mr. Lockwood who had never before been involved in the day to day running of a large mill[24]. Weavers were dismayed, for instance, by his ignorance when he constantly referred to looms as machines. Mr. A. Recalls how Mr. Lockwood tried unsuccessfully to have the looms readjusted to make them work faster than they were designed to do. His thorough going reorganisation probably saved the firm from bankruptcy in the early 1930s, but his regime resulted in a good deal of underlying resentment and discontent which still lingers on in people's memories.

TIME FOR AMUSEMENT

Though the problems of the '30s featured so prominently in interviews, former employees were keen that the good times as the mills as well as the bad should be recorded. There appears to have been a camaraderie particularly among the women which those in domestic work, for example, never experienced. The young adolescents straight from school would take the opportunity of any break in the work routine to provide their own entertainment. One remembers playing 'Sally Armies' with improvised instruments until an overlooker came along to stop the noise. Good use was made of lip-reading, which was essential for communication against the deafening noise of the machinery. On one occasion, after retailing a 'women-only' joke in this fashion, Miss J. was told by the overlooker that he too could lip-read! One of the young office workers who still lives to tell the tale, used to enliven his midday break by visiting the man in charge of the Grease Works. There the soapsuds used to clean the wool after sorting were treated, so that the grease in them could be extracted to produce a saleable bulk wax, used for example in candle manufacturing. Vitriol was used to 'break down' the soapsuds collected in large tanks and the boy had discovered that one or two drops of the acid could be added to water to make a fizzy drink 'just like lemonade'[25].

On Christmas Eve every year each section finished work early in the afternoon and the seasonal festivities began on the premises, which would have been suitably trimmed for the occasion. Food was brought in by the women and sherry or beer purchased from the contributions made over a number of weeks to the appropriately named 'fuddle fund'.

Holidays being so few in number were eagerly anticipated. Christmas Day and Boxing Day, Easter Monday and Whit Monday, two or three days in August and two or three for the Burley Feast in October were all the workers could expect before and during World War I. Gradually the holidays were increased so that the few days in August became a full week. Firms such as Fisons did not give holiday pay to their employees prior to World War II. Workers who wished to do so paid into a 'Thrift' fund in the '20s and '30s which they could draw out prior to the August holiday. For those who had been sufficiently

15. A day trip by charabanc organised by the Rifle Club to Blackpool in 1922. It seems to have been a typical summer's day in August!

'thrifty', a holiday away from home in apartments was possible[26] or day trips by charabanc might be preferred. The Rifle Club, to which many mill workers belonged, arranged many day trips at holiday times. According to the *Ilkley Gazette* Blackpool, Scarborough and Morecambe were the favourite resorts for Burley workers in August 1929[27]. In the early 1930s Burley mill holidays received little attention in the local press, apart from a notice in 1931 which referred to the 'Thrift' fund as being at its lowest for many years[28]. Up to World War II the annual shut down at Greenholme had an impact on the village as a whole, so

16. Mr Arthur Thorne (standing) was presented with a clock by Mr. J. Horace Lockwood (seated), chairman of Wm. Fison and Co., Ltd., to mark his retirement after 56 years in the pattern department, in March 1962. Behind is John L. Lockwood, Director. Photo by Wharfedale Newspapers

that the mill holiday week in early August, became the village holiday week.

CLOSURE OF THE MILLS

Some of those interviewed had worked, like Arthur Thorne, at the mills for 50 years and more by the time they closed in 1966. During that time they had witnessed a reduction in the numbers employed there and a reduction in the influence of the mills on village life. Some indication of the decline in the number of textile workers can be gained from the summary reports of the 1951 Census[29]. Burley had become a part of Ilkley Urban District in 1937, a Council which included Burley and Menston with Ilkley, and in the whole area only 203 textile workers were counted.

Under the chairmanship of J.H. Lockwood from 1932, the firm was intent on survival and shed any commitments which might have involved extra expenditure. The numerous cottage and shop properties which the Company owned were gradually sold off to raise capital. In the Land Survey carried out by Inland Revenue in 1910, 119 such properties were owned by Wm. Fison and Co. Less than thirty remained to be sold at auction in 1968[30]. The large stone built Lecture Hall, built by the former owners to encourage useful leisure pursuits and house the nineteenth century mill school, was sold to Burley Urban District Council in 1935. The grounds adjoining the mills with the path to the river Wharfe received less maintenance than previously and public access was denied to preserve the estate from 'trespassers'. This action of denying public right of way in 1934 led to Mr. Lockwood (who was himself the M.P. for Shipley until 1935) being challenged in the House of Commons by the local M.P., who had received complaints from the members of the Burley Conservative and Unionist Club. The Burley U.D.C. also protested in vain as the Company continued to enforce its property rights.

After World War II, with increasing foreign competition and lack of capital investment, Burley's mills continued to be run down until the village's industrial centre virtually disappeared. Burley's attractions as a residential area — already well known to the more affluent middle class commuters who had settled in the village after the coming of the railway in 1865 — were further developed with the building of new estates on the outer fringes to the south and west of the village. The mills were out of sight by the river, unseen by the majority of residents and the many who passed along the main road through the village.

17. A group of women from the former twisting department posed for this photograph in front of the burnt out buildings in July 1966.

From left to right they are: Doris Seed, Nellie Holgate, Annie Metcalf, Mary Hildred and Grace Thacker.

A serious fire on the premises in July 1966 made headlines in the local weekly press, when an arsonist caused a blaze in a block which contained the Cockatoo building. It had already become a storage facility for plastic plumbing equipment and the blaze utterly destroyed the large L-shaped block. (see illustration 22.)

The following pictures given to us by Denis Williams illustrate the extent of the damage which was caused.

FIRE FIGHTING: A 300ft high column of flame and smoke towered over Wharfedale in the early hours of July 5, 1966, as part of Greenholme Mills in Burley-in-Wharfedale was gutted by fire. At one point, 15 fire engines were at the scene, as the fire ripped through the warehouse of Valor Cisterns Ltd, plastic moulders. The heat was so intense that even one of the hoses being used by the fire brigade was charred.

18. The Cockatoo building ablaze (the Bradford Telegraph and Argus.)

19. A view from the roof of the surviving buildings of the damage.

The final closure of the textile mills, apart from a report of the auction when the reserved price was not reached, provoked no comment. The closure seemed largely irrelevant to most people in Burley and was just part of the evidence of Britain's industrial decline. The site was eventually sold by private treaty and divided into units.

20. Lunch time in 1910: one of the set of photos in the Greenholme collection held by Bradford Museums, Galleries and Heritage.

An advertising feature in the *Wharfe Valley Times* of 1988 listed the activities being pursued there including the manufacture of bean bags, electronic equipment, a research laboratory and speciality chemicals, advertising display units, kitchen fittings, textile machinery and designer knitwear[32].

"Worsted manufacture had no longer any place but lives on in the memories of those few survivors who remember working there" (Margaret Warwick in 1988).

21. The same roadway in July 1966.

The three photographs (20-22) show how the mills' fortunes changed in the last hundred years.

The fire destroyed the L-shaped block.

Cockatoo building

23. Plan of Mills: Photo viewpoint

22. A recent view, with the clock casement still in place.

BURLEY-IN-WHARFEDALE in 1851

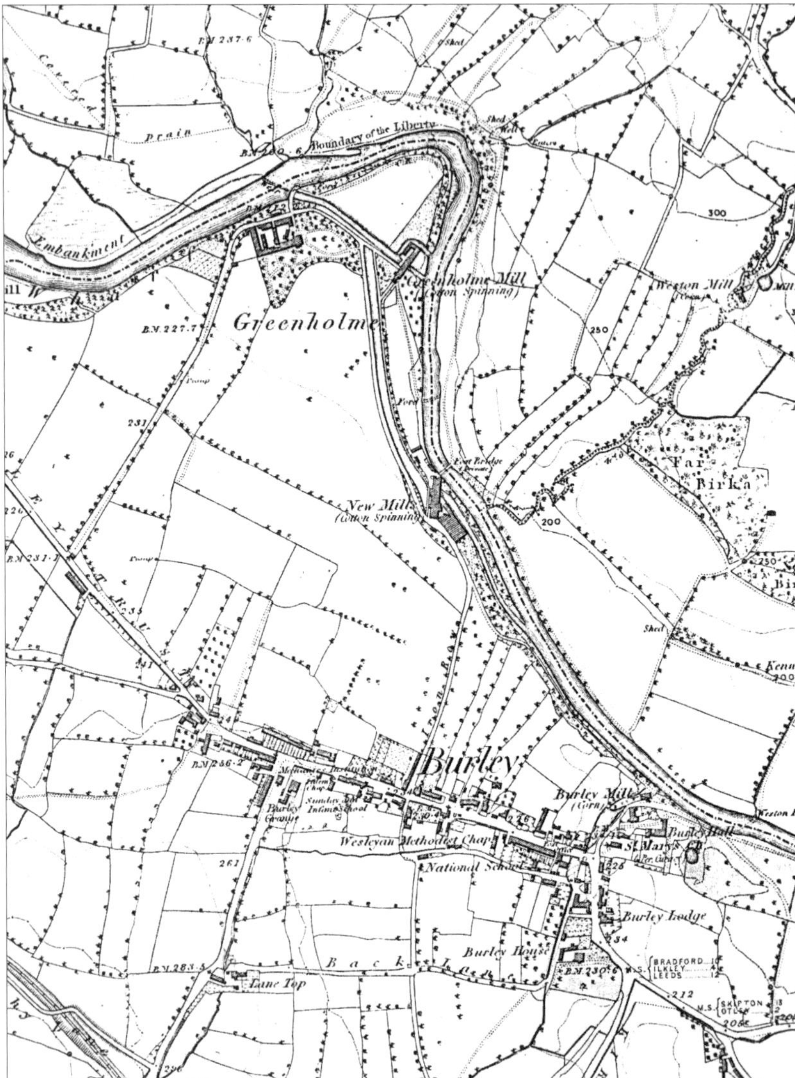

24. This is a section of the first six inch Ordnance Survey map of Burley-in-Wharfedale, showing the site of Greenholme mills, named Greenholme Mill (1792) and New Mill (1811). The village population was just under 1900 people, mainly in houses on Main Street.

BURLEY-IN-WHARFEDALE in 1901

25.The abandonment of the first mill and the extension of New Mill, now renamed Greenholme Mills is seen on this 1901 map. The houses at Greenholme and Wharfeside and the spread of buildings in the village have appeared. Burley had a population of over 3,300.

26. BURLEY-IN-WHARFEDALE in 1934

Further extension of the village can be seen in this map of 1934, but the house at Greenholme had been demolished. The mills could still provide work for over 450 people when the village population had grown to about 4000[33].

PART TWO

THE MILLS BEFORE THE FISON ERA

Close examination of the three previous maps shows how the whole village changed over the period following the formation of Wm. Fison and Company. Margaret did not include in her 1988 book the history of the village and its mills before 1850, but she had carried out extensive research into the earlier part of the nineteenth century and some of that was included in an article she published in *The Yorkshire Archaeological Journal* in 1971[34].

A detailed history of the first mills can be found in George Ingle, *Yorkshire Cotton 1780 –1835*[35]. He describes Greenholme Mill as "one of the most successful mills in terms of the length of time that cotton spinning was carried out on the premises." It had been started in 1792 by a partnership of Thomas Davison, George Merryweather and Jonas Whitaker. It was a five storey building run by a labour force of pauper children ("apprentices") brought from London. The partnership did not last very long. "Davison left the firm soon after the mill was built and the partnership between Whitaker and Merryweather did not appear to be amicable. The firm traded as Jonas Whitaker and Co....In 1810 George Merryweather took his share of the workforce and marched one hundred and ninety apprentice boys and girls to Manchester to set up business there." After Merryweather left, John Greenwood and Lister Ellis, two very experienced and wealthy cotton mill owners from Keighley, joined Whitaker..."

A further partnership was set up after this, which was bought out in a sale of the mills in 1819 by John Greenwood and Jonas Whitaker. The particulars of the sale have survived and this showed details of both the Old and the New Mill, each of five storeys, which were lit by gas and carried out both the spinning and weaving of cotton. The sale also specified several properties as well as the mills. These included the six lodging rooms for 142 apprentices, a large dwelling house, twenty brick built cottages at Greenholme, seventeen stone built, fire proof cottages (known then as New Row and now called Iron Row), several other houses and parcels of land in Burley.

The beginnings of cotton spinning in Burley depended on the existence of a power supply. This had been created by the construction of a dam across the river Wharfe at Greenholme. According to a pencil written document, which survived the fire among the files of the mills[36], the 1792 partnership bought the site of the mills and permission to erect a dam on the river from Sir James Ibbetson, owner of the Denton Park Estate, which at that time extended south of the Wharfe. They constructed a dam of wood supported by heavy stones and dug out the channel or goit which led the water from the weir to the mill wheels across the neck of the field called Greenholme (the land inside the bend of the river). A further goit was dug out to carry river water to the second mill (The New Mill) built some fifteen years later. It was about this time that the dam was swept away in a flood. A new more secure structure was constructed, known as the dams-

27. The weir with the boards still raised, following a storm.
This photo also appeared in the *Town and Country News* feature in 1927.

tones, which is there still (see photo 6). On top of that structure a line of strong wooden planks supported by iron rods and

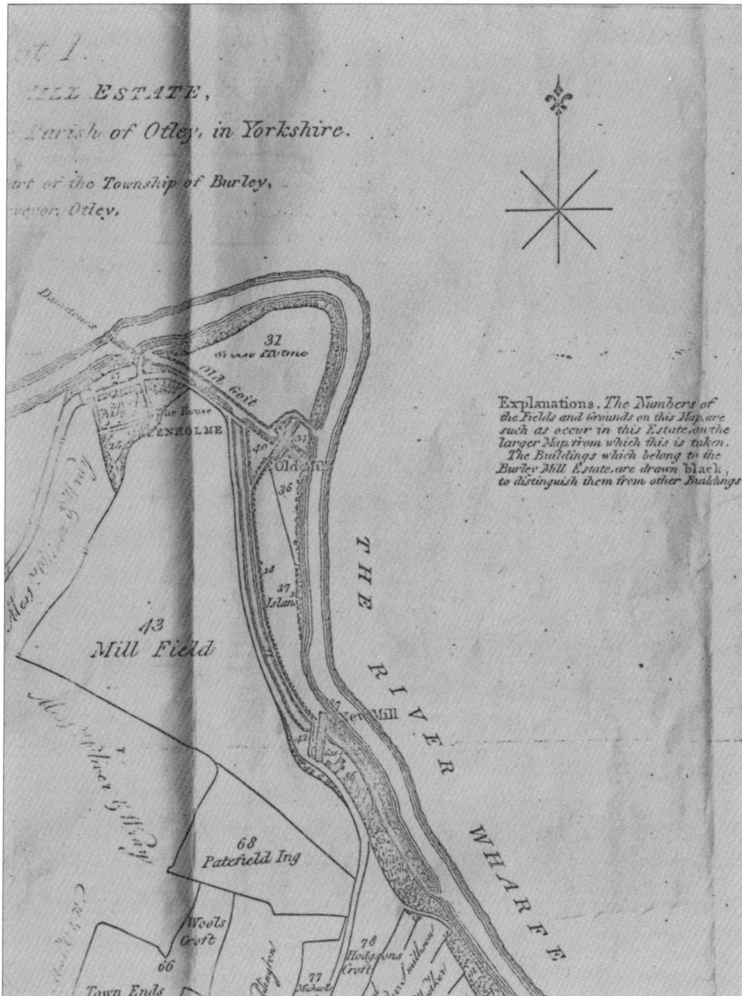

28. This unfortunately damaged plan was part of the particulars for the sale in 1819 of the Mill estate and its properties. The familiar bend of the River Wharfe can be seen with the "damstones" marked and the orginal house. The new damstones allowed water to be diverted along goits to the old mill and the new mill. Magnification of the new mill site, shows a building marked gas house, enabling lighting of the premises.

chains was placed in such a way that they could be raised to provide a greater volume of water in dry periods. They were lowered when the volume and flow of water increased after snow melt or heavy rain.

It was Lister Ellis who brought gas to the mills. He had the firm of Boulton and Watt construct and deliver the plant which would supply gas to 200 burners so replacing the candles which were the only source of light before this. The plant was constructed near the New mill built in 1811. It was further extended later in that decade, and this was to be the basis for lighting the whole village of Burley under the Local Board of Health in 1856[37].

The first partnership of Davison, Merryweather and Whitaker planned to have cotton spinning running round the clock, but they found it difficult to get workers to do night shifts. Indeed there was much unrest among those employed in the domestic textile industry, who saw great threats to their livelihood from the new textile mills. The Luddite protests, as they were known, never got as far as Burley, but the threat was such that alternative sources of labour were sought. Along with many other manufacturers at the time they decided to use children from orphanages, foundling hospitals and poor law houses.

George Ingle in his account of the Burley cotton mills, as we have already noted, refers to the "one hundred and ninety apprentice boys and girls" whom Davison took with him to Manchester when the first Burley partnership was terminated. In the same period of time, Parliament was persuaded that there was possible abuse and legislation was sought. This resulted in The Factories Act 1802, sometimes also called the "Health and Morals of Apprentices Act". Its purpose was to regulate factory conditions, especially in regard to child workers in cotton and woollen mills. It was the culmination of a movement originating in the 18th Century, where reformers had tried to push several acts through Parliament to improve the health of the workers and apprentices. The act had the following provisions:

- Factory owners must obey the law.
- All factory rooms must be well ventilated and lime-washed twice a year.
- Children must be supplied with two complete outfits of clothing.
- Children between the ages of 9 and 13 can work maximum 8 hours.
- Adolescents between 14 and 18 years old can work maximum 12 hours.
- Children under 9 years old are not allowed to work but they must be enrolled in the elementary schools that factory owners are required to establish.
- The work hours of children must begin after 6 a.m., end before 9 p.m., and not exceed 12 hours a day.
- Children must be instructed in reading, writing and arithmetic for the first four years of work.
- Male and Female children must be housed in different sleeping quarters.
- Children may not sleep more than two per bed.

On Sundays children are to have an hour's instruction in the Christian Religion. Mill owners are also required to tend to any infectious diseases. Fines of between £2 and £5 could be imposed on factory owners, but the Act established no inspection regime to enforce conditions. The act failed to provide a clear law of the hours one is permitted to work and failed to include supervision to make sure the law was being followed. Indeed Whitaker and Merryweather in Burley decided to campaign against the Act along with other local millowners. They invited a well-known Leeds surgeon, William Hey, to visit Greenholme to examine the health of the children working there[38].

The report shows that there were 260 apprentices resident at Greenholme Mill, all of them working in the Old Mill as the second mill was not built until 1811. Of these, 52 boys worked from 7 p.m. to 6 a.m. Dinner was brought to them at midnight, but the mill 'is not stopped' and 'they take it whenever the work is going on so favourably as not to prevent them from eating. After leaving the Mill at 6 a.m., they take what is to them a supper, and are employed till 10 in the morning, either in learning which is pursued in the winter season, or in summer in sportive exercises. They then go to bed and rise at 6 or 6.30 in the evening, and after their breakfast go to the mill at 7p.m.'. So they work 11 hours but there are 'many short intervals of rest'. The rest of the boys were day workers, with a shift of 12½ hours and ¾ hour for dinner. Hey reported that 'health of the boys does not appear to have suffered in any degree from their night work; but it seemed not so pleasant to the children, in general, as that of the day'. Work at night was lit only by candles at this time. Hey also noted that boys on night shift would probably continue on the same shift for four to five years. Whether accidents occurred is not reported 'yet no death has hitherto occurred amongst the night-workers' he said. Further, 'care is taken in the religious and moral training of the apprentices in this Factory'[39].

'On the strength of his verdict', the manufacturer contended, 'a repeal of the late Act, or a considerable modification of its obnoxious clauses, will appear indispensably necessary to the future success of a great number of persons embarked in the spinning and manufacturing of cotton; who have not only contributed largely to the public revenue but, at a heavy expense, trained them up in the habits of industry and religion, and tendered them (before, a load upon society) now some of its most useful members'. The report sounded convincing, but it happened to fall into the hands of a member of the Society for Bettering the Condition and Increasing the Comforts of the Poor, and a committee of enquiry was set up to investigate Hey's report. While recognising that the cotton industry was adding wealth not only to the manufacturers but also to the country generally, the committee felt that 'it is evidently cruel and unjust that the poor orphan, or the deserted child, should be *compelled* to do that night work, which the free labourer cannot, on any practicable or moderate terms, to be *induced* to undertake'. The committee's report concluded by suggesting that the manufacturers were virtually guilty of employing slave labour[40].

There is little mention of the girl apprentices except that they 'seemed uniformly healthy and happy'. From another source we know that **Rebecca Gregory** had been brought to Yorkshire from St. Margaret's Workhouse in Westminster, where she and her sister Mary had been placed when her parents had fallen on hard times. In 1797 at the age of 9, Rebecca became an apprentice at the mills along with her 10 year old sister. This we discovered when Gillian England from Wiltshire wrote in 2006 to tell us that her great, great, great grandfather, David England, a blacksmith at Greenholme Mills had married a second wife, Rebecca Gregory. Rebecca had a strong sense of religious belief and impressed many around her, so much so that after her death, someone unknown, possibly helped by Rebecca's sister Mary, wrote a long eulogy. This has been transcribed and a copy sent to us by Gillian England.

Much of the eulogy is a description of Rebecca's religious faith and how she put it into action, but it also includes some description of the situation of apprentices in the mills and how they came to be there. "As workpeople were required (in 1797) for the cotton mills at Greenholme two gentlemen were sent up to London to the Workhouse there to procure some young persons for Apprentices. They went to St. Margaret's and the Boys and Girls were ranged in a room for inspection. Mary and Rebecca were standing together and the latter was a small delicate looking Girl. Mary was selected, Rebecca passed by. The matron of the Workhouse, who had ever been a kind friend to them and had heard that their dying mother had wanted them to stay together, told Mary to stand aside....One of the gentlemen noticed this and remarked 'I have chosen that girl'. The matron replied, 'Sir if you have her you must take her sister likewise, it was their dying mother's wish they should not be separated. He immediately consented and they were brought along with many others in Yorkshire in August 1797."....Under the influence of John Whitaker, father of Jonas Whitaker, one of the partners in the mills, a strong member of the Wesleyan Methodists who spent much time with the apprentices, Rebecca "joined the Wesleyan Methodist Society...and became a member of John Whitaker's class in 1803." ....One of the overseers of the apprentices however forbad Rebecca (and all other apprentices in his group) from "going to the class meeting, threatening punishment in case of disobedience". She nevertheless went to her class – only one other had dared to do the same and "the next morning she was severely reproved and punished". However, Mr. Jonas Whitaker heard of this and sent for Rebecca. Though afraid of what might be in store, she was "sustained by peace and a consciousness that I had only done my duty". Whitaker's words soon relieved her, for he is reported to have said "I understand you have been suffering much on account of Religion. I wish to do something for you, you may have your choice of any work you like in the Mill, or if you prefer it you may come and be a servant in my house." With 'great joy', Rebecca accepted the position of servant in the Whitaker household, and remained in service with them for 25 years until she married the widower, David England, in 1828. She had no children of her own, but helped to bring up a son and two daughters of her husband. Rebecca died at Greenholme on 30th December 1858, aged 70[41].

Professor Katrina Honeyman of Leeds University has carried out extensive research into the use of pauper apprentices in the developing textile industries in the late eighteenth and early nineteenth centuries. "From the employer's point of view", she writes, " parish apprentices....seemed to carry all of the advantages of free child labour with fewer of the disadvantages....They came without parental baggage (so the employer did not have to find work for the parents or be concerned about their living accommodation)....An apprentice coming at age eight or nine, and surviving to the end of his or her term, provided a dozen or more years of unpaid labour. Upon release, he or she would be replaced by a 'new' apprentice. Such replenishment would take place gradually, because of the staggered timing of the apprentices reaching the end of their terms"[42].

All the children concerned, like Rebecca and her sister Mary, would have been put into the care of their home Parish overseers, who would have to find money from local rates to pay for their keep. So it was advantageous to the Parish overseers, too, to have the children taken off their hands. Indeed a premium was often paid by the parishes to the employers who took them, usually £4 or £5. The employers, or their agents, would be responsible for arranging transport by coach or wagon from the home parish to the employers' factories. The formalities of apprenticeship were executed properly, according to Honeyman, and the children were examined by magistrates and officers of the parish before consent was given for them to be handed over to the employers. Registers were kept by the parishes showing where the children were sent. The parish of St. Margaret and St. John, Westminster, from where Rebecca and Mary came, sent 36 girls and 32 boys to Burley in 1797, and over the next four years sent a further 32 girls and 30 boys[43]. At this time, Honeyman has calculated that nearly nine out of ten employees at the Burley mills were parish apprentices. Most came from London parishes, but there were also others from Leeds.

Professor Honeyman asks whether the reports of abuse and ill treatment of such apprentices were justified. Certainly the general literature of the day suggested that they were and this led to continuing campaigns for more rigorous control of employment of children in factories. Honeyman's research attempted to assess the treatment of apprentices. She finds that some parishes were more concerned than others to visit and check the state of children sent to factories by them. Similarly some employers were more considerate than others. Many children were exploited, abused and neglected and stories of runaway children testify to that. Sometimes however the apprentices were well-used and protected, and Honeyman found that the parish of St. Margaret and St. John, Westminster, seems to have been among the more concerned for their apprentices, while the Burley mills were thought to have created good conditions for their apprentices[44]. Rebecca and Mary possibly therefore were among the luckier pauper apprentices. Altogether between 1792 and 1816, the mills in Burley employed 143 girls and 117 boys from London parishes, and 17 girls and 17 boys from Leeds[45].

Rebecca, aged 63, born in London, appears in the 1851 Census records for Burley living with David England her husband, a blacksmith, aged 62 and Hannah Hird, a married daughter who was a power loom weaver. They lived in a cottage at Greenholme. The 1851 Census does not give place of work, but we can assume that Hannah was employed in the newly converted Greenholme mills by William Fison and partner, in worsted manufacture. The 1851 Census of Burley lists 34 women who had been born in or near London and for the most part married and not employed. Their ages range from 41 to 65 and it is possible that they were brought to Burley like Rebecca. Many of them had had children some of whom were working in textiles. It seems fair to assume that Professor Katrina Honeyman is justified in concluding in her book about child workers in England and specifically at Greenholme that the mills 'founded on the labour of parish apprentices, the enterprise eventually became self-sustaining in labour as the apprentices became adult workers and produced the next generation of young workers'[46]. It is noticeable however that there were only three men living in Burley in 1851 who had been born in London and now aged 53 – 61. One was an overlooker possibly therefore still working at Greenholme. We do not know any more about the boy apprentices whom William Hey examined in 1802, but possibly their children were still living in the village.

Hey's and other similar reports set in motion a long debate both in parliament and in the country at large about the conditions of workers in the manufacturing districts. In 1819 a Factory Act forbade employment of children under nine, but again there was no provision to make sure that the regulations were being enforced. In addition there were no birth certificates so that it was difficult to prove that a child was under or over nine years of age. A Royal Commission[47] was set up to look into the state of factories and employment practices in 1833. It reported extensively and once more the Greenholme Mills came under scrutiny.

THE FACTORIES COMMISSION, 1833

This Commission sent representatves to all the industrial districts in Britain, interviewing people at a sample of mills. One Burley witness to the Commission says that he went 'over to Leeds to induce (them) to visit our mill; we heard that you were not likely to come'[48]. Greenholme Mills wanted to be in on the act, for they were clear that they did not want the outcome of the Commission to be the imposition of maximum working hours. There was a movement afoot, led by Richard Oastler in West Yorkshire, to introduce a Ten Hour limit on all working in the mills. Whether or not they had intended to visit the Greenwood and Whitaker mills, the Commissioners came with their lists of questions to be answered. Three sets of responses are recorded in the published evidence, those on behalf of the firm, those given by Jonas Whitaker himself, and those of Thomas Brown ("thc prinicipal superintendent of the mill of Messrs Greenwood and Whitaker").

Twenty seven questions were put to the first representative of the firm, asking for details of manufacturing processes and sources of power, the number of employees, by age and gender, conditions of employment, pay, hours, shifts, absences, sickness, holidays and discipline, and the effect of proposed regulation of working hours. Jonas Whitaker had seventy nine questions put to him, but essentially they covered the same ground as those put to the earlier representative with the addition of probes into the relation of the firm and its employees to the law and the magistracy. The answers reveal that in 1833 there were 360 employees working at Greenholme in the two mills.

Age Range	Males	Females
Under 10	8	5
10 – 14	32	36
14 - 18	19	35
18 - 21	10	39
Over 21	45	131
	114	246

The hours of work were from 5 a.m. to 7 p.m. and there was no night shift other than for mechanics, who had to repair any breakdowns, and night watchmen. On Saturdays the spinning department closed at 3.30 p.m. but weaving continued as necessary for pieces to be finished. Among the youngest there were now no pauper apprentices, and all employees lived locally, or lodged with locals. In June 1818, there were 147 apprentices but by 1833 there was a sufficient supply of local labour for the mills. Just over half the workers were paid by the hour, and the rest were on piece work, that is, paid for completed jobs. Weekly wage rates for hourly workers varied from two shillings for the youngest to seventeen shillings for the older males and seven shillings for the older females. Piece work did not tend to give employees much more than those on hourly rates. There were no paid holidays, but there was no work on Christmas Day or Sundays. Workers had the option of taking a holiday at Burley Feast or Otley Feast, but if they did they were expected to make up time lost.

The witnesses laid great stress on the good health and discipline of their employees, and they drew attention to the fact that the employees had already expressed themselves clearly about their views of work at Greenholme in a petition presented to the House of Commons on their behalf by Lord Morpeth in

June 1832[49]. (There is no indication of who might have been responsible and why it was sent at that time but it is clearly concerned about the possible reduction of working hours.) It begins: 'That your petitioners have hitherto lived in comfort, have always been employed, and had regular wages whether trade was good or bad; are fully satisfied with the hours of working as now established; and that the general state of health of your petitioners is as good as any other class of persons who have to earn their daily bread by labour.' The petition states that an experiment was tried for a week when they only worked ten hours per day, the result of which led them to believe they would soon be unable to earn enough to pay their way, and would soon end in poverty. Further we 'have been treated with kindness and humanity...and have been preserved from committing those immoralities, crimes and misdemeanours which too many of our fellow creatures are guilty of.' They stress that none of the employees has been charged with felony, poaching, drunkeness or any crime. They enjoy long working lives and 'of 166 marriageable young women only two were delivered of illegitimate children'. Finally, they press their request that Parliament does not 'pass any measure which will restrict (our) present hours of labour'. They did not wish to be made paupers.

Other witnesses repeat the claims with evidence that what the workpeople have said is true and that the employers are reasonable, honourable men, who do not exploit their workers or deal harshly with them. Thomas Brown, the principal superintendent of the mills for 22 years affirms that, while in other mills harsh and cruel punishments might be used, there is no cruelty at Greenholme. 'It is about twenty years since corporal punishments were prohibited in our mill.' Bad behaviour and poor work might result in a child being sent home or a fine imposed. The Chairman of Otley Petty Sessions, Mr. J. Armitage Rhodes, on oath swears that the employees have committed no crimes, and he adds that he has visited the mills on occasions unannounced and has never seen any disorder there, only 'cleanliness, comfort, health and satisfaction'. If any unfavourable expression passed his lips, he says, it might have been that the women's appearance was rather too gay, but he realises that times have changed! A doctor, Dr. Shaw, also on oath, stated that the health and morals of the employees were superior to those in any district about them. Another repeated assertion is that the death rate at Greenholme was as low as could be expected. Of 218 workers in 1818 only 23 had died by 1833, of 306 workers in 1823, only 24 had died, and of 376 workers in 1831, only three had died. Further time off for sickness was never beyond expectation. The general impression they wanted to give was that Burley workers were industrious, never lazy, well disciplined and lived in as healthy work environment as was possible, given the knowledge that cotton fibres and dust could be injurious to health if inhaled over long periods. Dangerous machinery was given protective shields to avoid other injuries, they claimed.

As further testimony that there is a good cooperative spirit in the mills at Greenholme, Thomas Brown adds that the employees are thrifty and save from their earnings. Also 'several of them have shares in two shops, which they established in the village for the sale of provisions and clothes. The proprietors have no share or connection whatever with either of those shops; some of the overlookers have. There are about forty of the workpeople who hold shares. They are from the mill generally. One of the shops is one of the principal shops in the village. It is worth now a considerable sum. It was established in 1815 by the workpeople. They complained of the extortion of the neighbouring shops, and asked me to draw up some rules for them. The proprietors approved of this, and lent them £300, £100 of it without interest, to purchase their stock. They have long since repaid this money, and are doing very well.... The second shop was started on the success of the first. No means whatever are used to compel the people to resort to these shops. They intended at first to sell only to shareholders, but found it in their interest to throw it open to the public'[50].

The Rules of the Association are appended to the witness's statement, but give the date of establishment as 1818 rather than 1815. They run into 24 clauses detailing how the "*cooperative*" is to be run, officers elected, committees to be organised, general meetings to be held and rules about share holding. At no point is the word '*cooperative*' used but this is exactly what it is and of course predates the official start of the Cooperative movement in 1844, with the Rochdale Pioneers, by nearly thirty years. Unfortunately we have no other information about these early cooperative stores in Burley. Whether there was any link between the one founded in 1818 and the Coop store which was situated in Peel Place from 1890 is not known but it is unlikely. That later Coop used the premises of a former Methodist society chapel. Probably the early cooperative stores failed in the decade after the Factories Commission Inquiry when conditions of trade in the Cotton industry changed. Records of that have not survived. In the proposed sale of the mills later in 1848, there is reference in the schedule to two shops in Burley belonging to the mills estate, but they were leased at the time to named persons and not to the "cooperative".

As we have indicated, Messrs Greenwood and Whitaker, and their colleagues and employees, in giving their evidence to the Commission, were keen to take every opportunity to raise objections to the proposals for limiting hours of work. Whitaker in his concluding remarks to the Commissioners is recorded as saying 'we believe the contemplated Ten Hours Bill would be exceedingly injurious to the cotton-trade; the legislature no doubt wish to encourage health and morals, but if this bill becomes law the effects would be to destroy many water-mills entirely in rural situations in the country, and drive the trade into large populous towns, where the proprietors have little or no control over their hands, and where health cannot be so well promoted as in rural scenes'[51]. He is keen to show that he is not thinking solely of his mills in Burley, but for all proprietors of water mills, which 'are subject to many interruptions for want of water, and frequently impeded and totally stopped by floods. Our opinion on this subject may be taken as impartial, because we have a regular supply (from the River Wharfe); but we know that if the hours were confined from half past five o'clock in the morning to seven in the evening, as stated in the Ten Hours Bill, that many mills in summer could not run more that from six to eight hours a day....If the proprietors were to apply steam to obviate this inconvenience they would be subjected to a great expense of coal, water-mills being mostly at considerable distance from collieries.' He then falls back on to his own situation pointing out that purchase of coal would not be the only cost factor to be taken into account. They have to get the cotton to the mills and that involves expensive carriage from Liverpool or Manchester. Then there is growing competition from Europe and America. All in all, he avers, the passing of the Ten Hour Bill into law would be a disaster for the cotton industry and the country[52].

Jonas Whitaker was not successful in stopping the Ten Hour Movement altogether, though it was 1847 before an Act was passed that fully enshrined the Ten Hour Bill into Law. Acts of Parliament in 1833 and 1844 did enforce some limitation of hours on children's work, (children under nine could not be employed and those between nine and thirteen were limited to nine hours a day). They did introduce the requirement for some educational instruction and routine inspection of factories[53].

Jonas Whitaker was a leading member of the Wharfedale community, and a man of many parts. Unlike his father he was a member of the Anglican church, and played a big part in the building of St Mary's Church in Burley, being a major donor to the building fund, laying its foundation stone in 1841 and taking a prominent role at its consecration in June 1843. As well as being a millowner, he had a great interest in animal husbandry and was a co-founder of the Wharfedale Agricultural Society with other Wharfedale notables, such as William Vavasour, Walter Fawkes, Sir H.C. Ibbetson and Lord Harewood, in 1806. The Society was responsible for the Show which celebrated its bicentenary in Otley in 2009. Jonas was born in Burley in 1768

29. Greenholme Mansion built in 1820. It was pulled down in 1923.

and lived for some time in Burley Hall. He and his family moved to Greenholme, the Palladian mansion which he had had built, in 1820. Among his children was Fanny, who aged 33 married William Fison in 1846. Now in his late 70s it seems fair to assume that he would want to retire from running the cotton mills in Burley. Whether that was the reason or not, an auction of the Greenholme Mills was arranged to be held at the Talbot Inn, Bradford on 17th May 1848.

THE 1848 AUCTION AND AFTER

The particulars in the schedule for the proposed auction give considerable detail about the two cotton mills at Greenholme and the other properties and land which formed part of the estate. (Also included in the auction was a woollen mill at Hell Hole Gill, between Burley and Otley, but that is not our concern here.) The "Old Mill" was five storeys high and worked by a water wheel 16 feet 6 inches in diameter occupying a fall of 13 feet. The "New Mill" fire proofed and also five storeys high

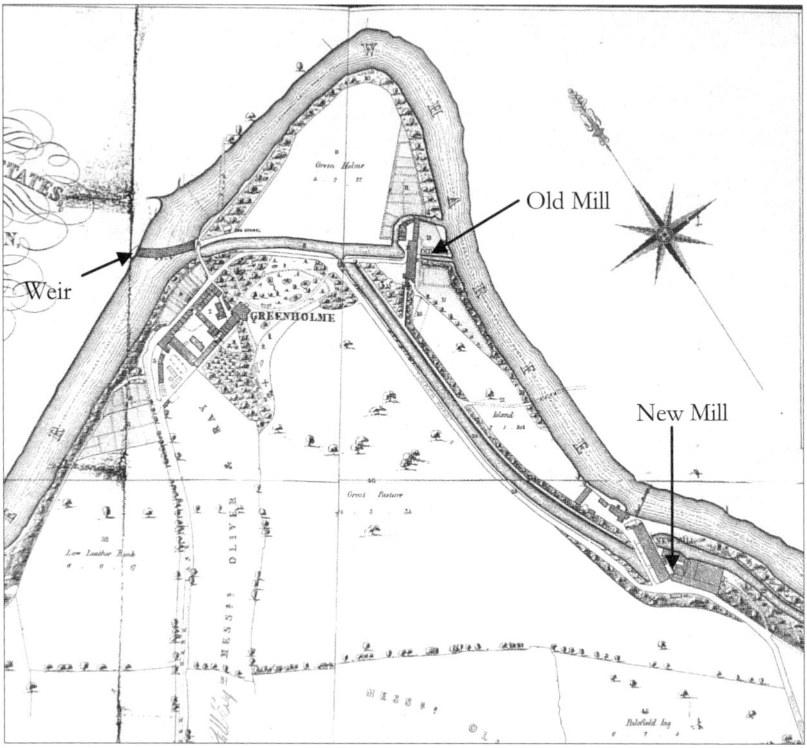

30. Part of the Estate plan published for the auction in 1848, indicators added.

was worked by two wheels, 30 feet and 22 feet in diameter respectively, both with falls of 19 feet. The larger wheel was also 18 feet wide, and was said to generate 146 horse power. Water supply was from the goits, which were regarded as being able to provide a constant flow of water to the wheels.

Apart from the mills, their machinery and fixtures, and the gas houses, there were parcels of land, amounting in total to

136 acres, the mansion known as Greenholme (which had eleven bedrooms), a farm and all its buildings, 23 brick and stone built cottages between the mansion and the farm, 11 cottages by the old mill, 13 stone built cottages forming Pleasant Row on Main Street, 17 stone built cottages, described as fire proof, forming New Row (now Iron Row), 7 other cottages elsewhere in Burley, a large dwelling house (with five bedrooms) and two shops in Burley. (These might have been the shops set up as "cooperatives" by the workers in the mills in 1818.) The cottages in Greenholme and by the Old Mill were home to nearly two hundred people, so no doubt there would be lots of speculation as to what was going to happen to them and to the mills. Burley was likely to undergo changes in any case, because in 1846 an Act of Parliament had been passed to allow the Midland Railway Company to build the Wharfedale Railway, which was eventually to connect Burley with Leeds and Bradford and the rest of the growing railway network. (The railway was not opened until 1865, but the prospect was there, as the Particulars for the planned auction stated)[54].

The auction failed to find a buyer for the Greenholme estate and so it was left to Messrs. Bentley and Wood, the solicitors in Bradford, to look for other possible purchasers. It was not until 1849 that a buyer came forward. There are varying accounts of what actually happened, but one that seems to have been written by a descendant of the eventual purchasers is perhaps true. This was published anonymously in *The Airedale and Wharfedale Observer* on 30th May 1930[55]. There it claims that after Mr. Whitaker retired from the business in 1849, Mr. Greenwood, his partner, intimated to William Fison, Whitaker's son-in-law, that the family would very much like him to purchase it, in order to keep it in the family. Fison was reluctant, possibly because of the cost factors such as those Whitaker mentioned in his evidence to the Factories Commission. Further, Fison was in the Worsted business, and to continue in that trade the Greenholme Mills would have to be completely changed from cotton manufacture. William Fison had been in business in Bradford with William Edward Forster since 1842, and Forster was more inclined to at least have a look at the mills. This they did but they decided that they would have nothing to do with the purchase. Fate is said to have taken a hand, however, for the very next day, two engines in their existing works in Bradford and Keighley broke down. This led them to change their minds and they decided to negotiate for the purchase of Greenholme Mills.

"Now comes the interesting part of the story. A letter was received [by Fison and Forster] from the solicitor stating that the property was on offer to Sir (then Mr.) Titus Salt, who had not then founded his great works at Saltaire. The solicitor intimated that Mr. Salt had arranged to see him before 1 o'clock that day, and if he did not purchase, then he would be prepared to negotiate. So at one o'clock Messrs Forster and Fison went to the solicitor's office, and finding the place not sold, they arranged terms, signed the agreement and were preparing to leave, when who should come in but Mr. Salt, who was prepared to increase his offer and purchase the property. Very much annoyed was he at being too late, but had he kept his appointment before one o'clock, Greenholme Mills would have belonged to Sir Titus Salt, and Burley might never have known either the right Hon W.E. Forster or Mr. William Fison"[56].

After this a great transformation of the mills took place. We have no information of what happened to the employees but 'the old cotton mills needed renovating and re-equipping for worsted production, and, on 7th August 1850, a sale of unwanted machinery was arranged at Greenholme...' No reference has been found to the purchase of new equipment for the spinning and weaving of worsted goods which the partners intended. However, a letter dated November 1850, refers to a celebration to mark the getting to work at the new mills[57]. The new owners sold their Bradford mills and settled in Burley. The Fisons moved into the mansion at Greenholme which would have been a homecoming for Fanny. William E. Forster was living in

Rawdon, and had married Jane Martha Arnold in August 1850. They decided on a site in the field known as Low Leather Bank and had a house built alongside the river, calling it Wharfeside. They occupied that in February 1852. According to Forster's biographer, Wemyss Reid, the capital needed for the mills' reorganisation influenced Forster to move from his large house at Rawdon to a 'more modest structure' at Burley[58].

Forster and Fison had invested in worsted manufacturing at Greenholme during a period which proved to be one of growing economic prosperity in this country. The business expanded considerably during the first ten years: in 1850 about 300 were employed there but by 1862 the figure was nearer 600. In 1851 there were 78 out of 294 heads of households in Burley employed as textile workers. In 1861 there were 119 out of 369 heads of households in textiles[59]. Most of the operatives needed were available in the village itself or the surrounding district, but Burley received numbers of incomers from surrounding areas. Most of these were from other parts of Yorkshire, especially the Dales, where lead mining was declining. One group of migrants, mainly members of five families, came from Wellington in

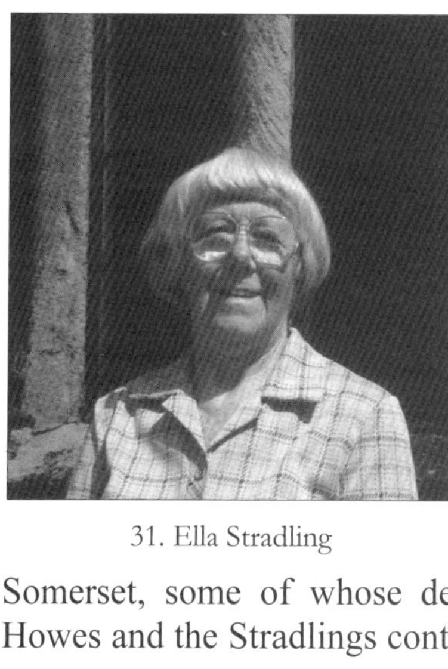

31. Ella Stradling

32. Mary Hill nee Stradling, d.2002

Somerset, some of whose descendants, like the Thornes, the Howes and the Stradlings continued to live locally[60]. There were very few Irish migrants or from other overseas countries, but there were four who came from India in 1859. They were the young Arnolds, Edward, Florence, Hugh and Frances, the or-

33. Hugh, Edward and Florence soon after arriving from India.

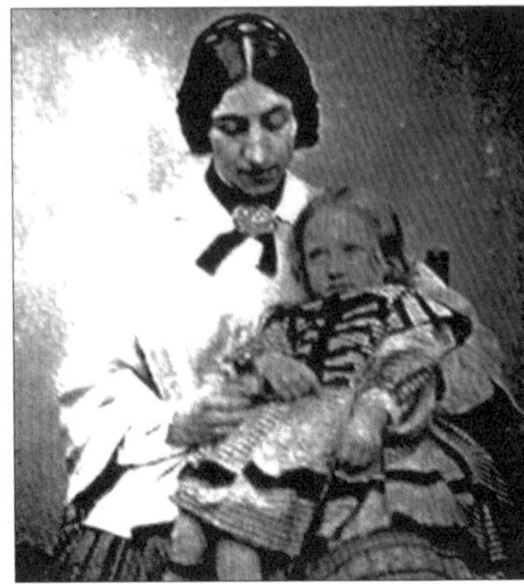

34. Frances, the youngest, with her Aunt Frances, sister of Jane.

phaned children of William Arnold who was brother to Jane, the wife of W.E. Forster. The Forsters adopted them and they later changed their surname to Arnold-Forster. One of them, Edward, became a director of the mills and Frances was the last of the family to live at Wharfeside. She donated the Fountain which stands at the bottom of Station Road[61].

Recruitment for mill work was no longer the problem which it had been in the early days of factory organisation, when it was difficult to find sufficient operatives willing to subject themselves to the harsh routine. Whereas [as we have seen] the first owners of Greenholme mills had imported pauper apprentices into the village to help swell their labour force, Forster and Fison inherited second and third generation workers fully accustomed to the rigours of mill life. Burley-in-Wharfedale, by their time, had developed into an industrial village with the livelihood of its people dependent on the Greenholme mills. Renewed activity there in 1850 and subsequent expansion must have been welcomed by many of the inhabitants.

That is the point where Margaret's original account began. Now it remains to complete the story.

POSTSCRIPT: RECENT DEVELOPMENTS

The decline of the mills which occurred in the 1930s and the brief revival of their fortunes with the Second World War is mirrored in the decline of the population living in Greenholme. In fact the population decline began earlier. There were 60 people living in cottages around the old mill site in 1851 and a further 121 living around the large mansion at the same census. By 1901 there were only 30 inhabitants including those at Wharfeside, which was built after the 1851 Census. The large mansion which the Whitakers and Fisons had occupied, was owned by the Fison company and until 1910 tenanted by Arthur Greenwood and his family. After that no tenants stayed long. Following the First World War domestic service was no longer attractive either, and the company decided to demolish the house and recoup as much as possible by the sale of the stone. Government subsidies were available for house building at that time and the company used the building materials in the construction of the eight substantial houses in Great Pasture. Apparently just before the old mansion was demolished, a large number of local worthies was invited to one last party at Greenholme, and the demolition began the following morning. A big flat stone taken from the portal of the old house was placed on the site as a memorial and it is still there today (see p.62).

Throughout the period from the late eighteenth century to the present, as the sketch maps show, the buildings at Greenholme have retained a remarkable rectangular pattern despite changing use and the recent rebuilding of the area to provide some 25 modern dwellings. It is almost as though they have been built to retain some historical shape to match an ancient site, but there is no evidence of any such history. There has long been a ford across the Wharfe at the bend, however, and it is

35. Greenholme Comparisons 1818 to 2010, compiled by Ben Plummer.

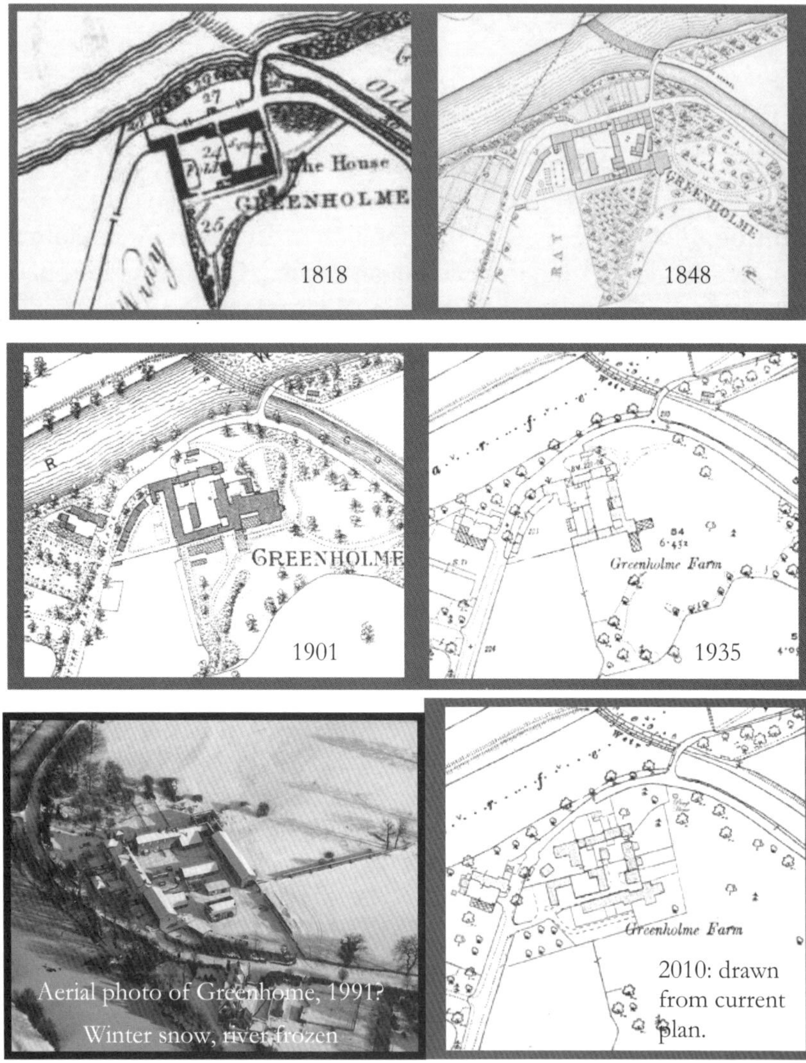

probable that a small hamlet would exist at that crossing point. It would have been a suitable point for cattle drovers from the north to cross on their journey to the towns and cities of the West Riding. No clear evidence exists however. The meadows near the river have always provided suitable grazing for livestock, and farm buildings have continued to be a part of the complex. When the cotton mills were first built it is probable that more accommodation was needed and certainly the pauper apprentices must have been housed near the old mill site. There is no indication, in any of the reports mentioned earlier, where such accommodation was situated. Today the fields at Greenholme are still part of an agricultural economy.

There is however a new development. Two companies in partnership, TLS Hydroelectric Power Ltd. and Derwent Hydroelectric Power Ltd. have combined to use the old mill site to generate electricity. They already have experience of and running hydroelectric power stations on such sites as that at Greenholme. They will use the water which is diverted from the Wharfe at the damstones, in a spillway which they are constructing at the eastern end of the original goit. The fall is sufficient to

36. The goit looking west from the site of the hydro project

37. The turbine housing under construction looking south east to the river.

drive turbines to generate enough electricity to meet the typical demand of 300 homes. The plan (over) shows where the turbine house will be and the photographs show the development taking place in August 2010. It is hoped to have the generators producing electricity by the Spring of 2011[62]. Water power was used to spin cotton in 1792. and now it will be used again to heat and light Burley homes in 2011. The industrial revolution continues?

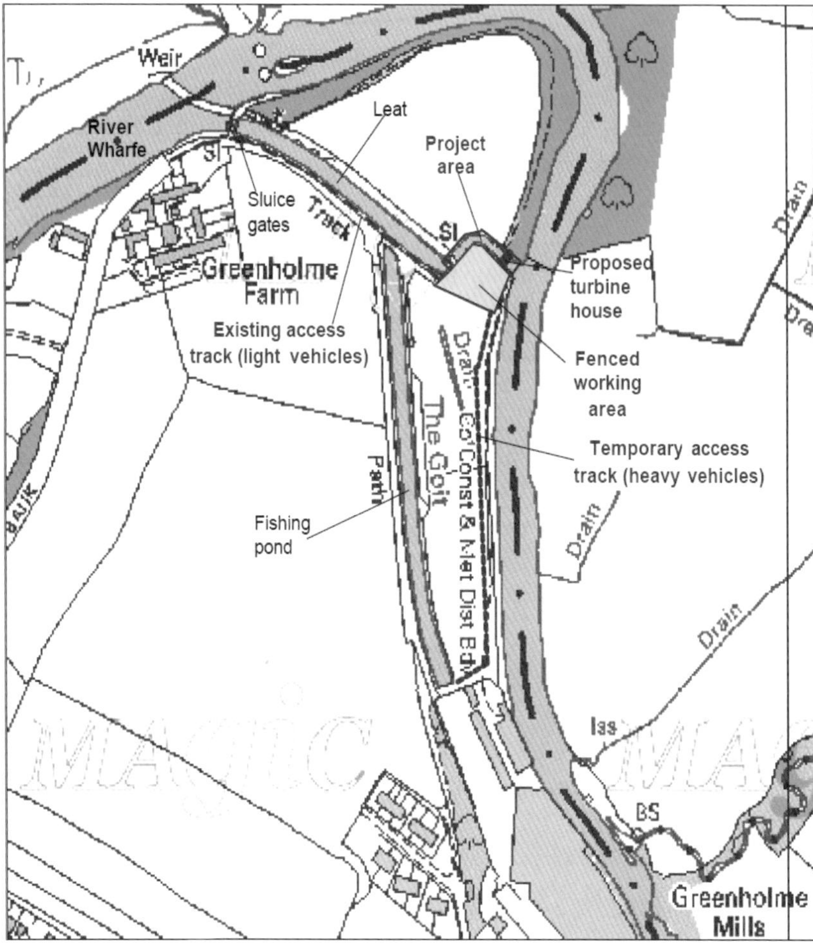

38.Sketch map showing the site of the Hydro project, supplied by Derwent Hydroelectric Power Ltd.

REFERENCES FOR GREENHOLME MILLS REMEMBERED AGAIN

1. Registrar General Census of Population 1851, 1861 1871 and 1881 Calculations based on the schedules for the two enumeration districts of Burley-in-Wharfedale which cover the main village. Burley Woodhead and Stead not included.
2 Registrar General. Census of Population.
Urban Areas with less than 20,000 population and Rural Districts: Occupations, 1921, Yorkshire, West Riding.
3 Census (ibid).
Urban Areas with Population not exceeding 50,000 and Rural Districts, 1931, Yorkshire, West Riding
4 Kelly's Trade Directories for the West Riding of Yorkshire.
5 William Fison & Co. Ltd., Minutes of Board Meetings, II. 1922 -65. March 9, 1927.
6 Ibid. February 12, 1932.
7 The 100 year secrecy rule forbade the release of census details such as household members names and ages. This rule has been relaxed for the 1911 Census which was available for scrutiny in 2009. Since Margaret's book was published the details for 1891, 1901 and 1911 have been released. In 1901 42 percent of the boys aged 12 – 15 and 33 percent of the girls aged 12 -15 were in textiles.
8 Registrar General, Census 1921.
9 Registrar General, Census 1881, In 1901, 186 women over 15 years of age worked in textiles, and of those only 11 were married.
10 Registrar General, Census 1921. In 1901, 20 percent of the adult males in Burley were classed as textile workers.
11 Registrar General Census 1931.
12 The pent was a marker indicating the point at which the 70 yard length was completed.
13 Various products manufactured at Greenholme are referred to in a pamphlet reprinted from *Town and Country News,* May 1927.
14 Committee on Industry and Trade, Survey of Textile Industries, report dated 1928.
15 The full length overall worn by male sorters.
16 *Ilkley Gazette* 24 May, 1929.
17 *Ilkley Gazette* 31 May 1929.
18 Registrar General 1931.
19 *Ilkley Gazette* 3 February 1933.
20 *Ilkley Gazette* 5 May 1933.
21 *Ilkley Gazette* 16 June 1933.
22 *Ilkley Gazette* 1 September 1933 .
23 Minutes of the Board, 21 March 1933.

24 J. Horace Lockwood (b. 1888 – d. 1972) was a solicitor and Conservative M.P. for Shipley from 1930-34. He resigned from the Conservative Whip in June 1934 and became an Indpendent Conservative until his defeat by the official Conservative candidate in November 1935.
25 The process at the Grease Works is described in the feature in *Town and Country News,* 1927.
26 Holiday makers rented rooms and bought their own food which was cooked by the landlady.
27 *Ilkley Gazette* 9 August 1929
28 *Ilkley Gazette* 17 August 1931
29 Registrar General Census of Population 1951: Industries. Burley is not listed separately after the formation of Ilkley Urban District Council in 1937.
30 The information about properties held in 1910 is held in the Registry of Deeds, Wakefield, in "Land Values: Inland Revenue (Finance Act 1909/1910) Skyrack Division, West Yorkshire. The properties for sale in 1968 were listed in the Sale Notice, *The Greenholme Estate*, Dacre, Son and Hartley, 1968.
31 Report of J.H. Lockwood. Minutes of the Board, 3 December 1934.
32 *Wharfe Valley Times*, 21 April 1988. There have been many changes since.
33 The summary records of the 1931 Census, give the population of Burley as 1942 males and 2219 females
34 M. Warwick, (1971) "W.E.Forster's Work in Burley-in-Wharfedale (1850-1886), *Yorkshire Archaeological Journal, Volume 43*
35 George Ingle, *Yorkshire Cotton 1780-1835*, Carnegie Publishing, 1997 pp220-225
36 The pencilled note referred was given to Margaret Warwick by the widow of a former mill employee, Mr. Frank Taylor, and can be seen in the Burley Archives.
37 This information was passed to Margaret in 1986 by Ken Golisti, of Leeds, who had researched the early gas industry in England and made a particular study of such records as were available for the Wharfedale area. He notes that the inhabitants of Burley were the first in the Wharfe valley to witness the wonders of "inflammable air" as gas was known in 1811. A copy of an unpublished paper on the Gas Industry by K.C.M. Golisti can be seen in Burley Library Archives.
38 See B. Inglis(1971) *Poverty and the Industrial Revolution*, London, Hodder and Stoughton pp.79-80
39 The report is contained in *Reports of the Society for Bettering the Conditions of the Poor*, Volume 4, London 1805.
40 B.Inglis (ibid) p.80.
41 Gillian England (2006) *Rebecca England (nee Gregory) of Greenholme, Burley-in-Wharfedale, 1788 -1858* Sedgehill Publishing, North Bradley, Trowbridge, Wiltshire.

42 Katrina Honeyman, (2007)*Child Workers in England, 1780–1820, Parish Apprentices and the making of the Early Industrial Labour Force*, Ashgate and Gower, London. p.7
43 Ibid. p. 77
44 Ibid. p.219
45 Ibid. p. 279
46 Ibid. p.109
47 *The Commission on the Employment of Children in Factories, 1833*, British Parliamentary Papers, Vol. 5 p. 32-3, 109-111 & 298-9, Irish Universities Press.
48 The evidence of Thomas Brown, 1833 op.cit.
49 The petition of working people employed in the cotton factories of Messrs Greenwood and Whitaker, 1833 op.cit.
50 The evidence of Thomas Brown, 1833 op.cit. p.11.
51 Jonas Whitaker's evidence to the Factories Commission, page 19. Op.cit.
52 Ibid.
53 'Factory Acts', *A Dictionary of Modern History, 1789 -1945*, 1962 p.121.
54 The particulars for the proposed auction have survived and can be seen in the Burley Archives by appointment with the Burley Library. They were donated by Arthur Thorne, deceased.
55 "How Fisons Came To Burley, Story of the Firm, Two Giants of Industry", *Airedale and Wharfedale Observer,* 30th May, 1930. A copy is available in the West Yorkshire Archives, Bradford Central Library, Ref 27D78/10.
56 Ibid. No dates are given for this transaction, but sometime in 1849 seems to be possible. Salt then focussed his interest to the west of Shipley and work began in 1851 to create the industrial village of Saltaire, now a World Heritage Site.
57 This is in a letter from Jane Forster to her mother, referred to in a footnote to M. Warwick, *W.E. Forster's Work in Burley-in-Wharfedale(1850-1886)* op.cit. Margaret when writing the article for the Yorkshire Archaeological Journal in 1970 noted that the location of Jane Forster's letters was not known, but later by chance a friend, Dr.Tim Jerram of Ilkley, visiting Dublin found many of them in the Archives of Trinity College, Dublin. See Margaret and Dennis Warwick, *Eminent Victorians, The Forsters of Burley-in-Wharfedale*, Burley Local History Group Publications, 1994.
58 M. Warwick, op.cit. 1971.
59 Census Enumerators' Books for Burley in the Otley Registration Sub-district for Wharfedale.
60 The five Wellington families, the Herrins, Howes, Stradlings, Thornes and Withymans came to Burley when the textile mills in Wellington were undergoing transformation. The mills there were owned by a Quaker family and it is possible that there was correspondence between them and the Forsters in Burley, though we have never found any.
61. See Margaret and Dennis Warwick, 1994, op.cit.
62. Information supplied in October 2008 by Derwent HEP Ltd.

ILLUSTRATIONS

APPENDIX

Memories of Greenholme Mansion (See illustration 29)

Margaret Warwick wrote this in the Parish Magazine, Christmas 1979.

The visitor who approached Greenholme House from the main drive in the early twentieth century would enter through the east facing porch with its solid round pillars. Once in the hall, his or her attention would inevitably be drawn to the grotto under the staircase, where water trickled gently over rocks amidst an elaborate display of ferns and water plants.

To the right and left of the front door on entering were huge double doors leading to the parlour on one side and the dining room on the other. Both rooms had full length windows facing east but the side windows of the dining room looked towards the river, whereas the larger side windows of the parlour looked towards the moors. From the hall access could be gained via the grotto to the conservatory, and from there to the south facing vinery and the gardens.

The kitchens and servants' quarters occupied a large area of the house and below them were the keeping, salting and wine cellars. Near the servants' hall, Arthur Hall, my informant*, vividly remembers the long row of numbered bells on springs which were connected to the bell pulls in the main rooms. Apart from the kitchen but just as necessary were the laundry, the dairy and the north west facing ice-house where block ice could be stored for culinary use.

Across the yard from the kitchens the range of buildings included a coach house, stables and a harness room. A family such as the Greenwoods, and the Fisons before them, would have two or three horse-drawn vehicles for their own use and others for farm and estate work. The extensive lawns were cut by a horse drawn machine, the animal wearing leather protective "boots" to prevent undue marking of the turf. A twentieth century development in the house at Greenholme was the electricity installation, designed to supply the main rooms. A small steam horizontal boiler to drive a dynamo was installed in one of the outhouses, and this, together with a supply of large sized wet accumulators, could produce sufficient electricity to light the main entertaining rooms.

Arthur Hall and his young friends would marvel at these electric lights when they went to the big house on Boxing Day each year. On these occasions the full staff of indoor servants, the butler, the housekeeper, the parlour maid and the house maid – to name but a few – were joined by the outside employees and their families. High tea was provided for 50 to 60 people in the servants' hall with the Greenwood family and their friends waiting at the tables. Games, competitions and carol singing round the illuminated tree in the hall, followed the feasting until the time came for the distribution of Christmas parcels. For the children there were toys or books and a small garment. The adults too had their parcels which might contain scarves, gloves or handkerchiefs, with chocolates for the ladies and tobacco for the men.

After Arthur Greenwood's death in 1910, Greenholme house and the estate ceased to be run in such a grand manner. The 1914-1918 war resulted in a shortage of servants and a changed attitude after that war towards life "in service". The house itself, built near to the mills for the Whitakers in 1820, was no longer so desirable a residence in the twentieth century when the tendency was for manufacturers to live at a greater distance from their works. When the Fison company could find no suitable tenant in 1922, a decision was made to demolish the old mansion and to re-use the stone for eight company houses at Great Pasture.

*Arthur Hall lived in one of the cottages at Greenholme as a boy, his father having a job on the estate.

39. The stone that marks the site of Greenholme Mansion, can be seen in the field between the new housing development and the path along the side of the goits. The inscription reads: "HERE STOOD GREENHOLME 1820—1923"

Ben Plummer.

ACKNOWLEDGEMENTS 2010

This account of Greenholme Mills has been based primarily on work done by members of the Burley Local History Group and the Tutorial Class which preceded it. In Margaret's acknowledgements the early members are named and thanked. I would like to add Jean Howson, Shirley Child, Suzanne Stracey, Lynne Foulkes, Bill Logan, Frederick (Bill) Howson and Harry Wise, who in recent years have been regular members of the group meeting to look after the archives on Tuesdays and Fridays in Burley Library. The archives there contain much of the material on which the book is based. Harry Wise sadly died in 2008.

I also thank Jane Cottle and the staff of Burley Library who have very generously put up with the Group. The archives are kept in the Library workroom and this has meant not a little inconvenience to the Librarians. Others in Burley have also made important contributions and thanks are due to Raymond Gill (who died in 2009), John and Yvette Horton, Brian Clayton, Ben Plummer, Mrs. D. Metcalfe, Gerry Shaper, Ella Stradling, Hilda Welbourne and Eileen Horton. Generally too I want to thank the residents of Burley who contribute to making this a wonderful community. Its history as a mill village is not forgotten, though for many it is now receding into the distant past, and for some this book may be a revelation. We need to remember it.

In preparing the text during 2010 I have consulted a number of sources which are listed in the references above. Many thanks must go to Professor Katrina Honeyman of Leeds University, for providing details from her research into the creation of an industrial workforce at the end of the eighteenth century. The account above about the pauper apprentices in Burley could not have been written without her help. Thanks go, too, to Alysa Levene of Oxford Brookes University who has also carried out much research on this early period of factory industry and has willingly communicated helpful information. In addition I want to thank John and Diane West who, through their personal connections with the site of the mills, have a fund of information and spent a morning telling me about their experience of Greenholme. The illustration on the front cover is from their collection of Greenholme memorabilia. Jamie Needle of Derwent Hydro - electric Power Ltd has kindly informed me of the current situation with regard to the construction of the turbine house which will generate electricity for the National Grid.

Above all, this book would not have been possible without the years of research that Margaret, my wife and partner of 54 years, carried out. Her meticulous approach to gathering historical information from archives and interviews with local informants, and her careful record keeping, led to the 1988 account and have made this addition possible.

It is my hope that readers will find it an appropriate memorial to Margaret whose sensitive and loving personality endeared her to many and whose legacy is inestimable. I am sure she would be glad that the additions have been made and that the proceeds are to be given to the Marie Curie Hospice in Bradford where she died.

Dennis Warwick   Burley-in-Wharfedale, September 2010.

40. The hydro electric power site in September 2010 looking north east towards the river. Photo by Ben Plummer.